Hurting Women

Patricia Russell

ISBN 979-8-89043-010-6 (paperback)
ISBN 979-8-89043-011-3 (hardcover)
ISBN 979-8-89043-012-0 (digital)

Christian Faith Publishing
832 Park Avenue
Meadville, PA 16335
www.christianfaithpublishing.com

Printed in the United States of America

Introduction

This book is the product of a prophecy spoken to me at a church conference in Waipahu, Hawaii, on May 8, 1997. I had no idea how it would come to pass, and I told the Lord I did not know where to begin. Praises be to God Almighty for a Christian woman, a sister in Christ, who was a member of our church during this time. She was on active duty in the Army and would be leaving us, and I did not want to see her leave Hawaii. While the prophecy was being spoken, she rejoiced along with me, although I did not know this until she was talking on the telephone that Saturday night, following the conference.

She was sharing with me that I had to get started on my book, according to the prophecy, and that she would help me. She gave me a timeline with a goal of one year to have the book ready for publication, which was to be May 1998, in time for the next year's conference. This was so I could say, "Look what the Lord has done."

After her praying and consulting with God on how to help me brings this book about, she told me the Lord had spoken to her on Sunday, while she was working at the chapel, that I was to write, and she would type. Although she was leaving, I did not know how this would be. She told me there is a mail system. She explained to me how it would come together.

During the Saturday night telephone conversation, the last hour was strictly prayer. The Holy Spirit had spoken to me through my sister's prayer language that there would be "more than enough."

This book is a compilation of three women who had suffered in very hurtful situations during their lives because they did not know how to get out. Yet they survived, now living to tell their stories, writing their stories, and proclaiming the message that it was for God's glory.

1960, the <u>hurting child</u>

I am the eighth child out of twelve. We all had different fathers. I was raised by my father and mother. My father had three children with my mom, one girl and two boys. My father raised my other siblings who were called stepchildren. Although I was not allowed to call the others "step," we were taught to call each other sister and brother. At the age of six, my family and I moved to New York City. I can still remember it. We were on a train "going up north." That is how the Southerners expressed traveling. We lived in Manhattan on 129, between Fifth and Lenox Street in a four-bedroom apartment on the fifth floor. I can remember my mother going to work in the mornings. Early in the morning, I could hear her crying because her feet were hurting so bad. My mother worked in a hotel that was many blocks away from my apartment.

In the mornings, before my mother would go to work, she would leave some change on the table for us, the younger kids. It would be 7 cents, 25 cents, just some change. In the 1960s, to us, that was a lot of money for a child to be able to go to the corner store to buy two-for-a-penny candy. The main reason why I did not like my mother leaving us to go to work is this one thing.

Later 1960s: <u>the abusive child</u>

As soon as my mother would leave the apartment, walk down the block, turn the corner, my brothers and sister would beat up my two brothers and me. I can remember when I was about five or six years of age, before we moved to New York, my oldest sister would force apart my legs, and beat me between my legs with a shoe. My oldest sister had a daughter at an incredibly young age. Her daughter and I were three years apart. My oldest sister would just bind me and let her daughter use her fist to punch me in the face. I always wondered, *Why am I being beat up so much?* There were no answers. As the years went by, my brothers and I would be beaten every day by our siblings.

Later in the sixties, when dope was so widespread, I could remember the older brother would mainline in the bathroom. Mainline means he would use a syringe to inject heroin into his arm or arms. I loved keeping myself and the apartment clean. I had just finished cleaning the bathroom when my oldest brother needed to use it. I went back into the bathroom to check after, to see if he was done using the bathroom and to see if it was still clean. My brother had blood running down the tub and the toilet! There was so much blood that I began to cry and scream and ask him, "Why would you use your drugs here in our home?"

He had put his hands around my neck and began to choke me. My sister ran toward us and began to scream out for our mother. She kept pulling on his hands and calling out his name. This episode would last approximately four minutes. She would call and scream out his name until he let me go. Then he finally dropped me to the floor. I would tell him that I hated him. When it was ending, I could feel myself fainting.

1960s: <u>the distraught child</u>

I used to daydream a lot, especially at night. My best time of the day was nighttime because it was peaceful and quiet. My mind would reflect on my oldest sister, how she would drink alcohol excessively. Sometimes, she would not come home. My mother would send my sister and me to look for her. We would find her at the bar or sleeping at someone's apartment. I would feel so bad when we found her. Her wig would be leaning on the side of her head. We did not know which was the front or the back to place it on her head properly. Her stockings would be all messed up. She would have a terrible body odor. I hated for her to talk to me because of her breath. So we got her home. She was always crying about something. I never knew what she would be crying about. She just cried about anything and everything. That was what I thought.

I could remember when my other sister would beat up my brother when she wanted him to go to the store. My brother was eleven years of age, and because he did not go when she wanted him to, she used her fist to punch him in the face repeatedly. We were always fearful in our home. We were too afraid to tell mother because they would beat up on us the next day. Whether we told on them or not, it did not matter because they would still beat us up.

My father was a hardworking man. He did not have a chance for education because his mother died at a young age. There were ten children in their family. He had to work on the farm. As years went on, the children were placed into foster homes. They were separated for a long time. I can remember, as a little girl, seeing my mother sitting at the table with my father, teaching him how to write his name and count money.

1971: *the pain of a sibling*

In October 1971, my oldest brother, the one I said I hated, was murdered on a nearby street corner. My brother was a dope dealer. I remember when he came home one day, and he put this roll of money in my hand and said for me to hide it. I said okay. That incident took place during the middle of the week. It was now Friday. He came home while my mother was sleeping. She frequently took naps. My brother said to Mom, "Why do you sleep so much?" He would frequently say to her, "I don't like you to sleep all the time."

The weekend passed, nothing new took place, but on Monday morning, I went to school. While I was in school, my emotions were estranged, and I did not know why. On that day, when school was out, I would take the train home. I would go uptown, get off at 125th Street, then walk five blocks down to 129th Street. On this Monday, I'll never forget it as long as I live. I saw my aunt and one of my oldest sisters who lived downtown. I was wondering, *Why were they here on a Monday? The only time we get together is on a weekend for a family dinner. It was so unusual for them to be uptown on a Monday!* That estranged feeling I had was getting stronger. When I got home, my father met me at the front door. I put my book bag down, and he said, "Tricia."

I said, "What is it, Daddy?" Fear was all over me.

He said my brother's name slowly. "Your brother is gone."

I said, "What do you mean he's gone?"

He said, "He is dead."

My mind flashed back to when I was wishing him dead. That day, I fell to the floor in tears. Daddy began to explain to me what had happened and comforted me. Mother had asked my father to go to the store for some coffee. As my father got closer to the street corner, he saw a young lady putting my brother in a cab. It scared him so badly that he ran back to the apartment up five flights of stairs. He began to tell my mother what he had seen. My mother began to put on her clothes to go to the hospital, and they took a cab to the hospital where my brother was taken. When my mother got there, they had just put my brother on a stretcher to rush him into the operating room. They had taken all his clothes off, and when my mother saw my brother, he had only a towel in front of him.

The money my brother told me to hold belonged to someone else. My brother was walking down the block, when two guys came to him and asked, "Where is the money?"

He said, "What money?" He had it, but he lied that he didn't have it. One guy pulled out a gun. My brother began to run down the block, screaming! I was told that money was flying everywhere as my brother was screaming out loud, "Somebody, help me, please! Somebody help me!"

There stood a crowd of people, but no one would help. My brother continued screaming for help. No one would help. My brother was a tall, slim, young man. He had a birthday that Saturday before his death. My brother was twenty-three years of age.

During this same time span, my younger brother was in a hospital for eye surgery. In our school, there were round metal disks on the four legs of the chairs. The kids would take them from the legs of the chairs, use their foot, and kick the disk down the hallway. The disk would spin and bounce off the wall. This day, my brother was changing classes, and when he turned the corner to go to his next class, the disk went into the air. My brother was wearing glasses, and the disk hit his glasses, shattered the lens, and the glass went into his eye. The doctors thought my brother would lose his sight or they would have to remove the eye. I cannot remember exactly how long my brother stayed in the hospital, but the next week, my oldest brother was killed.

My brother was buried, and my baby brother came home after the burial had taken place. My baby brother was about twelve years of age. I remember when he came home from the hospital. He was sitting in the den. He was asking a lot of questions. He always asked a lot of questions anyway. I was looking at him. He had a patch on his left eye. He asked where his brother was. I left the room because I did not want to be the one to tell him his brother was dead. The doctor told us to wait awhile before telling him about our oldest brother's death for fear it might put him into a state of shock. There were flowers from the funeral that was placed all around the house. He kept asking questions about his brother. My mother could not take it anymore, so she told him that his brother was dead. He cried so extremely hard. It hurt him to cry, and pain was already in his eye.

Time continued as my mother had to visit the doctor concerning her emotions and distress because it became exceedingly difficult for her to go past that corner where her son had been killed. She became so distressed she could not take it any longer. She spoke to her doctor about the stress she was having. He told her that she needed a change from where she lived. That was extremely hard for my mother to accept because moving to New York City was going to be that change for her, leaving from down South. Father was giving us a better life. The doctor said it would be best for her health that she moved back down South. She was told New York City is a fast city to raise children.

In Need of a Christian Home

I can remember at the age of sixteen, out of nowhere, Mother just said that we are going to church. What a church! Every time I went, I fell asleep or took the money that was given to me. I went to the store and bought candy.

They would always have a bake sale down in the basement of the church. I didn't know Jesus Christ until I was eighteen. There was not any Bible study in the home or living any kind of Christian life. *Proverbs 22:6* talks about training a child in the way they should go. My training was gossiping and lying, drinking, drugs and sex and fighting. That becomes a part of any child's life at an early age of his or her life.

But at that time in my life, it was a lot of bitterness and hurt, so we did move back down South. I did not want to go back down South. I wanted to stay in New York City. If you look at it, that is all I knew because I was six years old when we left North Carolina, and now I was sixteen. But there was something about growing up in a Christian home with two Christian parents. With not having a Christian foundation in the home, the path that I took was not in God's will. Just because I didn't drink or do drugs doesn't mean that I wasn't doomed for hell.

A Girl Named Deborah

*The fruit of the righteous is a tree of life;
and he that winneth souls is wise.*

—Proverbs 11:30 (KJV)

*The Godly are like trees that bear life-giving
fruits, and those who save lives are wise.*

—Proverbs 11:30 (NLT)

This scripture is proof of the life that Deborah lived. I met her in high school. She was in my homeroom class. She was incredibly quiet in school, didn't say too much, but I knew that there was something different about her life. We both were in the ninth grade. At that time of my life, something devastating happened that any teenager of my age should not have to go through. The bad thing about it was I had a lot of hate inside of me because of my brother's death.

It was a hot summer day in 1973. I was about eighteen years of age. I just had my first child. I was going shopping one evening when I saw Deborah. We began to talk about the past and what we are doing now since we graduated from high school. We did a lot of laughing about our school days and where our lives had taken us. Then she asked me if she can come see me sometimes.

I told her yes. After a couple of visits, Deborah and I became the best of friends. That was when she began to tell me about Jesus Christ. That he died on the cross for my sins. She also told me that he saves and forgives, and Jesus Christ will fill me with the Holy Ghost and that He is a healer. The only thing that I heard was that He is a healer. That was because I had asthma as a child growing up. I began to ask her questions about God healing me of my sickness. So she told me about *Isaiah 53:5*, and it says, "For he was wounded for our transgressions, he was bruised for our iniquities: the chastisement of our peace was upon him; and with his stripes we are healed."

Now that I am older, I always notice in the Word of God that this scripture fits everything in a nutshell, even though I wanted to know about His healing.

But God's Son was bruised for my iniquities which is my sin and the chastisement of all the beating that he took and the stripes and long strokes or blows with a rod just for me that day I am healed.

It is good to know that there are still other Deborahs out there sharing the Word of God. Now that time went on with Deborah teaching me the Word of God. I became a Christian. I got down on my knees in my one-bedroom apartment, alone in 1973, and invited Jesus Christ into my heart, for He had changed my life.

At that time, my husband was in the military, and it was time for us to go to a new duty station. Deborah was born in New York City.

While we tried to stay in touch, with both of us being young mothers, raising our family was hard. At that time, Deborah did not have a telephone, so I would call a friend to see how Deborah was doing. This was a young lady that came into my life that God profoundly changed.

I was really being used by God in witnessing, having Bible study in my home, leading Bible study at the church that I attended.

I so much wanted to let her know what God was doing in my life, but it seemed like every time I try to reach her or talk to someone that knew her, I would get the feeling that something is being hidden from me

So I stopped calling and just began to pray for Deborah.

This was a friend I could never forget. Not a day goes by that she wasn't on my mind. Even in my witnessing, I will tell others my testimony of how I became a Christian and the impact that this young lady made in my life, and I thank God for her that she kept right on coming, giving me that good news of Jesus Christ. Amen!

A Call for Prayer

In 1 John 5:14–15, it says, "And this is the confidence that we have in him that if we ask anything according to his will, he heareth us. And if we know that he hears us, whatsoever we ask, we know that we have the petition that we desired of him."

Petition—an earnest request

In 1988, my husband was stationed in Hawaii. I received a phone call from a friend. She told me Deborah was in the hospital. Deborah had cancer, and she was dying. I found out that she backslid (turned away from God), went back to the clubs, and committed adultery for five years.

And now Deborah was leaving me. I had a lot of questions for her, and I needed answers. She told me about the man that she was having an affair with and that she told him that she was leaving him.

He told her that she cannot leave him, that he would put roots on her (witchcraft), and that she would have to stay. Deborah was afraid of witchcraft because her mother used to work at the roots. I believe that God was bringing Deborah out of what she was in, and it would take a mighty God to do such a miracle. In the year 1993, my husband and the family moved back to Hawaii. I received a phone call from Deborah, letting me know that she was in the hospital, and she had been going through some chemotherapy. She sounded very weak and very tired. We talked for a long time on the phone. Deborah seemed to have some regrets because of the choices that she had made. She had some fears but was not afraid of dying. She said to me because of what was spoken over her life, she found herself believing it. That morning, while talking to her, I felt genuinely concerned about Deborah while listening for God's direction in what to say to her, waiting for Him to tell me what I wanted to say to my friend that I have known since high school. I wanted to make sure that I would say the right thing, and that she would be comforted.

If you knew Deborah like I did, she was always a strong and positive young lady. Extraordinarily strong in the world, she has helped me in so many ways. Spiritually, I was not going to judge her for the mistakes that she made. But I was on the phone to support her, she was my mandrel now it's for me to be there for Deborah. The devil tells lies to all believers, paints a beautiful picture like it's okay to do what we do.

John 10:10 says, "The thief comes only to steal and to kill and to destroy. I have come that they might have life and have it to the full" (NIV).

As we walk this life, the enemy will do everything that he can to destroy us. Now all the teaching that I have learned from my friend, it was time for me to remind her what God says in His Word. I prayed for Deborah that day, with tears running down my face very quietly; and I told her how much I loved her. I asked Deborah if she would like to give her life back to God. She said yes that day. I had her repeat after me *the Sinner's Prayer*, and she did. Before I got off the phone, I told Deborah that I would see her in heaven. She told me that she loved me also. When we finished talking on the phone, I continued to pray and weep for my friend. The next morning, I received a phone call telling me that Deborah had passed.

Second Corinthians 5:8–9 states, "We are confident, I say, and willing rather to be absent from the body, and to be present with the Lord. Wherefore we labor, that, whether present, we may be accepted" (KJV).

While I was in prayer, God spoke to me, and said, "She led you in the kingdom but did not know that it was ordained for such a time as this for her." God planned that I will be the one to lead her (rededicate), Deborah, back to the Lord. I lifted my hands up and began to worship the Lord with thanksgiving, knowing I would see my friend again.

She is deeply missed.

During the Storm

They mount up to the heavens; they go down again to
the depths: their soul is melted because of trouble.

—Psalms 107:26 (KJV)

No matter what kind of storm may come your way,
there is always deliverance. A pastor once said, "You may be
heading for a storm or coming out of a storm. No matter
which one you are in, it's how you come out of the storm."

When trouble comes in your life, you can always depend
on God. Some storms may be in a dry place, meaning I feel
all along' empty inside 'I do not know what to do or you can
say you can I turn to. Other storms: you may say will the rain
every stop.

Meaning I can't stop crying, I cry myself to sleep, my
eyes are swollen, I don't want to face my family or friends,
and I will just keep on pretending that everything is okay.

Mark 4:37 says, "And there arose a great storm of wind,
and the waves beat into the ship, so that it was now full"
(KJV).

Some storms will come out of nowhere that you were
not expecting. The waves feel like it is overtaking you. Just
like the disciples, they were used to the water. It was their
occupation. They were fishermen. The wind and waves came
upon them so fast that it filled the ship. When trouble comes

your way; stress, you are mad, you don't understand, why me and you began to feel depressed. Life feels like it's just beating you down, and you feel full of anger.

Luke 8:23 says, "But as they sailed he fell asleep: and there came down a storm of wind on the lake; and they were filled with water, and were in jeopardy" (KJV).

When you have Jesus with you, there is not a storm you cannot overcome.

When the disciples saw they were in jeopardy, they cried out for help. That's what we must do: cry out for help!

Jeremiah 33:3 states, "Call unto me, and I will answer thee, and shew thee great and mighty things, which thou know not."

Which Woman Are You?

"I wear a mask."

I am a yes woman. Never could say *no*! Low self-esteem has always played a part in my life.

Walking in fear, she will smile, then talk. Or just joke around to take the pressure off, 'Who you really are.

Never would show my real feelings, "whether you are an adult or young adult; or maybe you are a teenager."

Sometimes it's easier to wear a mask.

John 8:36 states, "If the Son therefore shall make you free, ye shall be free indeed" (KJV).

Romans 6:22 says, "But now being made free from sin, and become servants to God, ye have your fruit unto holiness, and the end everlasting life" (KJV).

Standing in the Shadows

Sometimes we find ourselves standing in the shadows of life when no one is looking, watching others going about their everyday lives, hoping that someone sees us. This shadow is a gray, lonely, cold, and dark shadow with no one to talk to, praying that someone will speak and just say hello. Maybe it will bring me out of what I am going though. Just to have someone to talk to may help or someone will just give me a smile. I see them, but they don't see me.

I woke up this morning with praise on my lips, just a small song that one of my songstresses/mentors had sung time and time again.

> *You deserve the glory and the honor.*
> *I lift your holy presence, and I bless your holy name.*
> *You deserve the glory and the honor.*
> *I lift my hands and worship and bless your holy name.*

There comes a great peace and calmness that the Holy Spirit brings when I know that the Lord is in my presence. I spoke to the *Lord* and asked what to do next. I am waiting on you, Lord. I will never do anything on my own.

In a Secret Place of a Woman

He that dwelleth in the secret place of the most High shall abide under the shadow of the Almighty.

—Psalm 91:1 (KJV)

There comes a time into every women life whether or not she has or hasn't experience, Depression, Loneliness, Abuse, Rejection, Suicidal, Bitterness and forgiveness. Or just raising her family and now the empty nest is now facing her. There are hidden doors that she has come to the reality that she forgot that was there, until she looks around one day and notices what about me.

Now the full circle has come back around, and all I see is but me. She fulfilled her dreams in motherhood where she carried all titles and responsibilities as wife, mother, teacher, counselor, friend, and so on. There is a secret place in every woman's life that she must face.

Tap one

<u>Loneliness</u>
Suicide

John 14:18 states, "I will not leave you comfortless; I will come to you."

When your life seems dark, and you may feel like there is no one to reach out to, you are surrounded by Jesus Christ's love, for there is hope.

Matthew 27:5 says, "And he cast down pieces of silver in the temple, and departed, and went and hanged himself."

There is so much that can happen in someone's life that can push them over the edge. Judas was used by the devil to betray Jesus. It may be a friend, Families, or the cares of this world, seeking help, we all need someone to talk to.

Comment:

Tap two

Abused
First Corinthians 6:9–10 says:

> Know ye not that the unrighteous
> shall not inherit the kingdom of God?
> Be not deceived: neither fornication, nor
> idolater's adulterers, nor effeminate, nor
> abusers of themselves with humankind,
> nor thieves, nor covetous, nor drunkards,
> nor revilers, nor extortioners shall inherit
> the kingdom of God.

God expects holiness from us. Unrighteousness should no longer be a part of our lives.

Comment:

Tap three

Rejection or rejected.

Jeremiah 8:9 sates, "The wise men are ashamed, they are dismayed and taken: lo thy have rejected the word of the Lord and what wisdom is in them?"

Do not let worldly wisdom make you reject the Word of God. There is comfort in the Word of God, not man.

Comment:

Tap four

Aging (praying, concerning)

Psalm 71:9 says, "Cast me not off in the time of old age; forsake me not when my strength failed."

You may disagree it is a beautiful thing to age. Yes! We have our aches and pains. It is the grace of God because we see our children grow up, and we see our grandchildren. And when that time comes, we have our children for support.

Comment:

Tap five

Image in the mirror (made in the divine image)

Genesis 1:27 states, "So, God created man in his own image, in the image of God created him; male and female created him."

There comes a time in our lives we investigate the mirror, and we see disappointment, hopelessness, sorrow. But when we realize that we are created in God's image, it gives us hope and faith.

Comment:

Tap six

Virtuous women (wisdom and virtue)

Proverbs 11:16 says, "A gracious woman retains honor: and strong men retain riches."
Proverbs 12:4 states, "A virtuous woman is a crown to her husband: but what makes ashamed is a rottenness in his house."
Proverbs 14:1 says, "Every wise woman builds her house: but the foolish plucked down with her hands."
We women can make our home or break it. We must call on God to help us build a joyful and righteous home.

Comment:

Tap seven

First Kings 17:13 states, "And Elijah said unto her, Fear not; go and do as thou hast said: but make me there of a little cake first and bring it unto me and after making for thee and for thy son."

Fear (blessing in the journey of life)

Today we are looking for jobs. It is hard to keep food on the table. A dollar does not go far anymore. The economy is not like it used to be. But if we obey God's Word by putting our trust in Him, we need to pray like never before. God can take what you have. It will become more than two fish and five loaves of bread.

Comment:

Tap eight

Friends
Friendship (friendship divine)

Proverbs 18:24 says, "A man that hath friends must shew himself friendly: and there's a friend that sticks closer than a brother" (His name is Jesus).

John 15:15 states, "Henceforth I call you not servants; for servants know not what his lord did: but I have called you friends: for all things that I have heard of my Father I have made known unto you."

Sometimes we expect friends to be there for us, but that cannot always be the case or they may change up on you. But there is a friend that is strictly closer than any brother. His name is Jesus.

Comment:

Tap nine

Death

Roman 5:1 says, "Wherefore, as by one-man sin interest into the world, and death by sin: and so, death passed upon all men, for that all have sinned."

It is an exciting thing to know, just because we were born into sin, and know that sin brings death, but how great it is to know that we have eternal life through Jesus Christ.

Comment:

Forgiveness (do yourself a favor and forgive)

Matthew 6:14 says, "For if ye forgive men their trespasses, your heavenly Father will also forgive you."

We must all do ourselves a favor and forgive because it lets us know when trouble comes our way and someone harms us in a bad way, if we don't forgive; we want to be forgiven.

Comment:

Tap ten

Marriage (commended)

Hebrew 13:4 says, "Marriage is honorable in all, and the bed is undefiled: but whoremongers and adulterers God will judge."

God created the first married couple, Adam and Eve, and He is pleased with man and woman in holy match monies, anything else is undefiled; and He will judge.

Comment: Never be unequally yoked with an unbeliever.

Second Corinthians 6:14 states, "Be ye not unequally yoked together with unbelievers: for what fellowship hath righteousness? And what communion hath light with darkness?"

Teenage Pregnancy

I remember at the age of seventeen, how I felt being pregnant: embarrassed, ashamed, afraid, and alone.

Sometimes as teenagers, we find ourselves in a place where we think we know it all.

What I mean is we don't even know who we are yet, being silly teenagers, girls not knowing what our young body is all about.

Yes, we have learned about health education in school. It is just curiosity. No! We know we're no way near maturity. Not even close.

At that time, parents didn't really educate us. I remember when I came on my menstrual cycle at the age of eleven. That was in the sixties.

My mother said to me, "Do not let the boys feel on you." That was my 101 education. Black and Hispanic women have the highest teen pregnancy rate (117 and 107 per one thousand women aged fifteen to nineteen respectively). Studies show that Whites (forty-three per one thousand) and Asians (twenty-three per one thousand) have the lowest rate of pregnancy before the age of fifteen to nineteen years and has been declining since 1991. Now the global adolescent birth rate from 2021 was about two births per one thousand girls aged ten to fourteen and forty-three births per one thousand girls and young women aged fifteen to nineteen.

Teen pregnancies carry extra health risks. Why should I save myself before marriage? Why should I save sex for marriage? When God creates something, He creates it with purpose and design. The Genesis account of creation makes it clear that God's creation is "good" (Genesis 1:31).

But mankind has a history of distorting what God has made, whether out of ignorance or only plain stubbornness. The golden calf (idol) of the Israelites, for example. Gold is beautiful to look at, but God clearly did not want His people worshiping it. Sex as God's idea is no different.

God created it, and therefore it is reasonable to expect that it is good. But when man distorts it by ignoring God's specific standards, it becomes harmful and destructive.

So, the question we have asked, "Why save sex for marriage?" is really a question of understanding God's purpose and design for sex.

We can choose to do things God's way and experience the beauty of His plan or we can choose to do things our way and experience harm and destruction (Proverbs 16:25).

So let us talk first about why God created sex. One reason is obvious: procreation. When God told Adam and Eve to "be fruitful and multiply" (Genesis 1:28), they probably figured out that He wanted them to have sex.

But God also wanted them to develop intimacy with one another, and He knew that sex would help them do that in a way that nothing else could.

God also knew that because sex is so powerful in creating intimacy that there must be some constraints on how it was to be used, so He specifically relegated sex to the arena of marriage.

The kind of intimacy that God desires between a married couple cannot occur between one person and several others. It can only be experienced between one man and one woman.

Hence God has specifically said, "Do not commit adultery" (Exodus 20:14), and "Flee sexual immorality" (1 Corinthians 6:18). That is, do not have sex with someone who is not your spouse. Obedience requires that sex be reserved for one's spouse.

So far, we have two basic reasons to save sex for marriage: (1) God tells us to, and (2) God's purpose and design for sex cannot be fully achieved any other way.

Many, though, have argued that extramarital sex is not all that harmful. Let us look carefully at the potential consequences for this area of disobedience.

Sex outside of marriage causes damage in at least two areas: (1) physical consequences, and (2) relational consequences.

The physical consequences are becoming increasingly obvious and increasingly dangerous today. AIDS and other sexually transmitted diseases are frightening realities. "Safe sex" is more accurately described as "reduced risk sex."

The only truly safe sex is abstinence. There is also a very real risk that children could be born and possibly grow up without two parents. Your actions affect your life, your partner's life, and the lives of your family.

They can result in handicapping an innocent baby's life as well. Worst of all, the willful destruction of human life often results from premarital sex. The relational consequences are just as real, though they may be more difficult to grasp.

First, sin always damages a person's relationship with his God.

Psalm 66:18 says, "If I had cherished sin in my heart, the Lord would not have listened." Intentional disobedience of God's command to not commit adultery dishonors and displeases God.

Conversely, God is pleased when His children chooses obedience and self-control, instead of the immediacy of pleasure. Second, relational damage happens between a Christian and those who are watching his or her life.

The sin of adultery (televangelist scandals) causes a person's friends and even "outsiders" to view the adulterer as less committed to obedience and more prone to hypocrisy.

But a Christian who saves himself or herself in obedience to God wins the respect of those who see his or her life. Sex outside of marriage also damages the relationship between the persons involved.

Trust is the main issue here. If two people do not cherish sex enough to wait for a marriage commitment, how can they trust one another for fidelity? Conversely, a man and woman build trust and respect for one another when they both survive the struggles of self-control. Each will have the confidence that the other respects them and cherishes their intimacy.

Similarly, if a person has not carried sexual purity into marriage, his or her marriage relationship is affected by the past. If a man or woman has previously had sex with someone else, their marital intimacy has already been affected.

One or both spouses will have to deal with real or perceived comparisons with former lovers and feeling that intimacy was not important enough for the other person to wait for it.

But if both have waited for their wedding night, the intimacy has already begun with a solid foundation. Why save sex for marriage? We have discussed several reasons: (1) God commands us to, (2) God's purpose and design for sex can only be achieved within marriage, (3) and the physical and relational consequences of sex outside of marriage are painfully real.

"But we're in love!" some might say. Maybe so, but if one believes in God's definition of love, he must realize that love is patient and kind; it does not seek to please itself nor does it delight in evil but is always hopeful (1 Corinthians 13).

True love would be patient in waiting for the proper time for sex. It would be kind to future spouses by not pre-harming marital intimacy.

True love would be unselfish in placing God's desires and the needs of others above itself. It would not delight in the evil of disobedience nor would it force another to disobey God.

Love could never be a reason for premarital sex; rather, it should be one of the greatest reasons to avoid premarital sex.

"But we're going to be married anyway" is another common excuse. Along with being presumptuous, this stance will almost certainly leave one question unanswered: If one gives in to moral temptation before marriage, what is to stop him or her from giving in to moral temptation once married?

"What if it's too late? What if I have already forfeited my sexual purity?"

Good question! Certainly, a person cannot reverse the past, but there are several steps one should take to keep from further damaging his or her intimacy with God and others.

First, acknowledge your actions as sin. For those who have accepted Christ's payment of the penalty for their sins, He asks only that they confess, agree with God that they are sinful. Second, maintain purity from this moment forward.

Jesus told the woman caught in sexual sin to "go and sin no more" (John 8:11).

You cannot change what has been done. I'm a witness. But you can keep yourself and others from any further damage by avoiding situations which might cause you to compromise your commitment to sexual purity.

Paul advised Timothy to run away from temptation (2 Timothy 2:22), and Joseph is famous for running from moral danger (Genesis 39:7–12).

Third, be honest with anyone who is a "potential spouse." Do not wait till your wedding night to discuss your sexual past.

Some intimacy problems may be averted if you address them early on. Sex is a good thing. It must be if God created it! The only way to keep it a "good thing" is to follow God's guidelines. God will reward you if you choose to honor Him and save sex for its proper time and place. Amen.

It's My Time!

I was in church last Sunday. My pastor was, preaching on "More' he was coming from. Chapter Matthew 1:4–11. The chapter was talking about how the devil came to tempt Jesus in the wilderness. He would say to Jesus, "Make these stones out of bread." You see, Jesus was fasting, and he had been fasting for forty days and nights, and Jesus was hungry. The enemy is always going to come and try to tempt our flesh. You know why? That is where we live. In our flesh. Jesus is letting us know that we can be overcomers in our flesh. Roman 7:18 states, "For I know that in me (that is, in my flesh,) dwelleth no good thing: for to will is present with me; but how to perform. that which is good I find not." When it is your time, you will know it, for your season has turned. The excitement, the joy of moving forward, in the next chapter in your life.

I Have Come to My Senses

My daughter just had a birthday not too long ago in 2016. These are the words she shares on her Facebook post:

> As I sit in my quiet time reflecting on how good; God has been to me. I`m thankful for His mercy: and His Grace, He grated me. daily, thankful for all the painful lessons I've learned; and the things I have gone through. Which made me who I am today. I am thankful for all the tears I have cried, and all` sunny days He has shone in my life. Next year of life I know God is ordering, my steps the more and granting me favor. In this year as I continue to Worship in praise and bring all my titles into the storehouse, that there may be meat in my house. God will continue to prove himself and open, the windows of heaven and pour out all the blessing he has for me. I am reminded daily, to be content with Him over these years. I've learning to put my trust in the Lord was easy. By no means will I ever think or say, I think, I am perfect, but by continual being. Faithful to Him, I know

He`ll continuously be, Faithful to me.
This is my special day, and I just wanted
to say thank you Lord for letting, for letting me see my 42nd birthday.

By Latricia

You Are not Defeated

There is a time in every woman's life that she feels like Job—**"The Thing I Fear the most has come upon me."**

College girls that are now ladies fear date rape. And maybe some have been raped and never told they have been taken advantage of. Women that are in the corporate world get less pay than men.

Single moms work two jobs to put food on the table and to pay their bills or to put their children through college.

Job 1:1 says, "There was a man in the land of Uz whose name was Job; and that man was blameless, upright, fearing God and turning away from evil." Job had seven sons and three daughters. And Job had seven thousand sheep and three thousand camels and five hundred she asses and a very great household so that this man was the greatest of all the men of the east.

Continuing reading the book of Job.

The point that I am trying to make is Job 1:8, and it states, "And the LORD said unto Satan, Hast thou considered my servant Job, that there is none like him in the earth, a perfect and an upright man, one that feared God, and eschewed evil?" (KJV).

So, the devil did stricken Job with sickness; children killed everything he owned was now gone.

Why do you think the devil didn't destroy Job's wife? Because there is one thing the devil will say: "I will save the best for last. The person that is the closest to you!"

In Job's suffering, Job's wife says to Job, "Why don't you curse God and die?"

Job says to his wife, "You sound like a foolish woman." What Job is saying is you sound like a doubting woman forgetting what God has given and done for us.

There are so many women who don't support their husbands when they are down and out.

Not just being an ungodly man, I am talking about a godly man too! God calls Job an upright man. That means he is a righteous man.

So don't be like Job's wife—not speaking in love, not supporting your husband.

Colossians 3:18 says, "Wives, submit yourselves unto your own husbands, as it is fit in the Lord." I say keep a clean heart and a clean mind in everything you do.

Somethings Comes by Fasting and Praying

You know, sometimes, in our life, we experience hardship that leads us to say, "God, I need your help!"

You know that there are things in your life that you yourself cannot fix in your own strength.

Why? We are human, and those burdens are too hard for us to carry.

This is when we reflect on the Word on God.

Mark 9:29 (KJV) states, "And he said unto them, this kind can come forth by nothing, but by prayer and fasting."

Jesus is letting us know that complaining in our own human flesh will not remove the problems, disappointment, sickness, depression, bad relationship, feeling suicidal, not knowing your identity. Look for answers by going to the Word of God. Jesus also teaches on moving the mountains out of your life.

Mark 11:23 (KJV) says, "For verily I say unto you, that whosoever shall say unto this mountain, be thou removed, and be thou cast into the sea; and shall not doubt in his heart but shall believe those things which he saith shall come to pass; he shall have whatsoever he saith."

Jesus is teaching us that mountains, being a huge rock, can be intimidating by looking at the size of it.

But (Faith), because the authority that we carry, only in God; letting us know to speak the word out loud, we can have what we will.

By speaking to what we are concerned about, that seems like it cannot be moved but it can make me believe in the Word of God. Hallelujah!

But God! Let us do a praise dance right now! To God be the glory. There is a song named "Hallelujah." Look it up and listen to it on YouTube. It got me through some rough times.

Now That the Son Is Shining

I don't know about you, but I can feel the Son shining by feeling His presence. You say, "How do you feel His presence?" I can be singing, praying, reading God's Holy Word, when you are fellowshipping with other believers, or just looking at God's creation. This is a sidenote.

You Are on Your Way!

2018, will be your assignments, that has been passed out; from the Throne Room' Of God. This year will not be any different than what you are already familiar with. Just keep going, pushing into your assignment you are carrying in your spirit that God birthed out of you. There will be obstacles that are designed to stop you! God has already put His Word in you.

James 4:7 says, "Submit yourselves therefore to God Resist the devil and he will flee from you."

Before you were conceived, before the day of your natural birth, there was a Word of prophecy spoken in you that your Creator Himself spoke to your spirit.

Jeremiah 29:11 states, "For I know the thoughts that I think toward you, Said the LORD, thoughts of peace and not of evil, to give you an expected end."

So your heavenly Father, God the Father, prophesied these words, living words, future words, words of hope. Accept your assignment, do not repeat tomorrow, disaster. Come on! Let us take our assignments seriously and with passion.

We are barking on the miracles of healing, revival of souls. *Take on your assignment. You know what it is.*

On the Threshing Floor

I had an encounter with the *Lord* this morning. I felt His presence so strong in my house I began to make my way to my family room.

It was so powerful that something that was so familiar to me, I began to do.

I took hold of my pillow and a washcloth, and I laid on my floor.

I began to pray with repetitive prayer, over some things that had hurt me to the core. I mean, true repentance. You know what I mean. That ugly cry, that I am so sorry cry, that cry from the gut.

Have you been hurt by your family and you begin to question yourself, saying, "I really thought we were family"?

Well! Let me tell you this. The enemy will use the closest thing to you. *That's family* (Genesis 2:23)*!*

The personality of Eve is as complete as that of Adam. In primitive intellectual and moral transactions, she has shared equality with Adam and is equally involved in their results. Different physical consequences fall on her for transgression because she is "woman, the mother of all living" (Genesis 3:16). But Adam doesn't escape retribution for sin, and it may be that the burden did not fall hardest on him (Genesis 3:18, 19), for motherhood has its joy as well as its pain in the companionship of newborn child-life; but the wrestler for subsistence from a reluctant earth must bear his hardship alone.

It cannot but be that much of the primitive conjugal love survived the fall. In that fall, sin began. There we were born into sin. *But God!*

I thank God for the second Adam (His name is Jesus).

So while I was down on the threshing floor, my God began to talk to me. He began to say, "I am going to make your year easy."

I said back to the Father, "Easy or easier?"

How many of you may have asked from God some clarity?

I continually pray in my heavenly language. Then He said, "I am equipping you for the equipment." (*Hallelujah*)

Then the Father said to me, "I will call you for a conference (face-to-face)!"

After God finished talking to me, it was a long conference call between me and God. When I got up off the threshing floor, I went into my office to search out what He had said to me.

A. *Conference*: this word is particularly used to express the grant of favors, benefits, and privileges to be enjoyed or rights which are to be permanent; as to confer.

B. On one of the privileges of a citizen, to confer a title or an honor.

1. Easy: "Whether is it easier to say to the sick of the palsy, thy sins have forgiven thee; or to say Arise, and take up thy bed and walk?" (Mark 2:9).

You see, I have been in chronic pain for three years without complaining. When I got off the threshing floor, I was healed. Hallelujah! I can go! Preach the Gospel without being in pain. Go to God with truth! Repentance.

2. Walk: "That's like as Christ was raised from the dead through the glory of the Father, so we also might walk in newness of life" (Romans 6:4).

3. Equipping: Ephesians 4:12, 13 (ESV) says, "To equip the saints for the work of ministry, for building up the body of Christ, Until we all attain to the unity of faith and of the knowledge of the Son of God to mature manhood, to the measure of the fullness of Christ."

4. Arise: Ascending; moving upward; originating or proceeding; getting up; springing up; appearing.

Launching, pushing ahead, never stopping, springing in your New. You have been told you are nothing or you will never be anything.

There is greatness inside of you. You are more than a conqueror (Romans 8:31–39) in Christ Jesus. Keep pressing forward. Don't give up and don't look back.

It's especially important to obey God. But the only way to obey Him, you must know the voice of God. Let's continually seek God's face.

It's Time to Let Go!

It took me the longest to know how to let go. What I mean about that is we can get so close to people or loved ones—yes, I said loved ones—that we tolerate everything or allow them to say what we really don't agree with.

Well, I'm glad you asked. When we put all our might and strength into a person, wanting the best for him or her, wanting them to reach their goals, it can be spiritual or just life itself. Whether supporting with finances, your time, counseling, praying, it's like they turn into this other person. Who are you? What changed you?

I woke up early this morning with God on my mind. I have been talking to God. I asked Him, "God, how do I let go?" You know when you always want to do for others.

I think my problem is I never know when the assignment will be over. I am the kind of woman that I thinks I'm supposed to keep on until all is well with the person.

So you don't know if you are the one who plants or the one who waters it significantly; but God, who keeps everything growing, is the one who matters.

So the words of God are saying, even though you are doing your best in what you do, we are not God, and we cannot outdo Him. It doesn't matter what we are doing for others from a real heart; everything we do, keep God in everything. And don't get tired of doing what is right.

So I thought I was putting too much water on the assignment and didn't know when it was time to stop watering.

How to let go? God is all significant, so let's get out of God's way.

So that same morning, I said, "God, teach me how to let go. Let me know when the shift comes."

He spoke to me that morning, from His Word in Ecclesiastes, chapter 3.

How Do I Let Go?

Ecclesiastes 3:1–8 says:

> There is a time for everything, and a sea-
> son for every activity under the heavens:
> a time to be born and a time to die,
> a time to plant and a time to uproot, a
> time to kill and a time to heal,
> a time to tear down and a time to build,
> a time to weep and a time laugh,
> a time to mourn and a time to dance,
> a time to scatter stones and a time to
> gather them,
> a time to embrace and a time to refrain
> from embracing,
> a time to search and a time to give up,
> a time to keep and a time to throw away,
> a time to tear and a time mend,
> a time to be silent and a time to speak,
> a time love and a to hate,
> a time for war and a time for peace

Let go of your past, let go of the hurt, let go of the unforgiveness, let go of the pain and the disappointment. Move on and enjoy life. Know your calling in God. And move forward in your next new assignment. Philippians 3:13–14 states:

> Brethren, I count not myself to have apprehended: but this one thing I do, forgetting those things which are behind, and reaching forth unto those things which are before, I press toward the mark for the prize of the high calling of God in Christ Jesus.

Knowing what's the important valuable part that you play in the body of Christ. The most important thing is doing the will of the Father, rather than what people think about you. Believe it! I know. I've been there. Hallelujah!

What Part Do You Play in the Body of Christ?

Paul is telling us in 1 Corinthians 12:14–25:

> Even so the body is not made up of one part but of many.
>
> Now if the foot should say, "Because I am not a hand, I do not belong to the body." it would not for that season stop being part of the body.
>
> And if the ear should say, "Because I am not the eye, I do not belong to the body." it would not for that reason stop being part of the body.
>
> If the whole body were an eye, where would the sense of hearing be? If the whole body were ear, where would the sense of smell be?
>
> But in fact, God has placed the parts in the body, every one of them, just as he wanted them to be.
>
> If they were all one part, where would the body be?
>
> As it is, there are many parts, but one body.

The eye cannot say to the hand," I
don't need you!" And the head cannot say
to the feet," I don't need!"

On the contrary, those parts of
the body that seem to be weaker are
indispensable,

And the parts that we think are less
honorable we treat with special honor.

While our presentable parts need no
special treatment. But God has put the
body together, giving greater honor to
the parts that lacked it,

So that there should be no division
in the body, but that its parts should have
equal concern for each other.

If we look at our natural body, if we have a toothache,
that one tooth makes the whole body hurt. You are going to
take something to stop the pain because it is like you have
not known comfort until that one tooth has been taken care
of. The body is not made up of one part, just the eye or hand
or the head. *All* are important.

For the body of Christ, every part is needed. You have
heard of the saying, "There's no little I! No little you." And
you have heard the saying, "One is a lonely number."

God wants us to come together, work together, for the
body of Christ is the head.

First Corinthians 3:6–9 (NIV) states:

I planted the seed, Apollos watered
it, but God has been making it grow.

So, neither the one who plants nor the one who waters are anything, but only God, who makes grow.

The one who plants and the one who waters have one purpose, and they will each be rewarded according to their own labor.

For we are co-workers in God's service, who are God's field, God's building.

In the Midst of Your Hurt

Why? Love hurts. *Love* is a strong word and a word of action. We can take the word and misuse it. How? Influence, capacity to influence a person's life. Just by studying their character of who do you wish to control? If you are not healthy in who you are, you will always find yourself chosen by the same kind of person. It was 2017 in the fall. I saw him. He still looked the same, very handsome. I had not seen him since middle school. We went to the same school. He was one of those bad boys, you know. Everyone knows, and your mom says to stay away from him because he was known for his reputation. He saw that it was a windy day. My hair was blowing in the wind; I was trying to press it down, but it did not work. He still had that same smile that would have melted any girl's heart.

We had a lot of catching up to do. We went for long walks and to the movies and dined out. I felt like I could have a future with this guy. He asked me if I was dating anyone. I became his girl. He would always wine and dine me. I never felt so happy. I had always heard a lot of things about him, but I always give a person the benefit of the doubt. Well, he began to change; his smile was not there anymore. He began to do a lot of shouting, and then he began to hit me. I loved him, and I thought things would get better. Our relationship lasted about three years.

On the streets were some rumors about my boyfriend. I never thought it was true. I guess they were true because he had to do some prison time. After a while, he was in and out of prison. I also looked at it as my way of escape. I know what I did was wrong, but I can go back to my roots where my grandmother was always speaking God's Word to me. First Corinthians 10:13 (NIV) states, "No temptation has overtaken you except what is common to mankind. And God is faithful; he will not let you be tempted beyond what you can bear. But when you are tempted, he will also provide a way out so that you can endure it." I guess we all can learn from our mistakes. For me, I had to learn the hard way. After my hard lesson, I decided to go to college; something I thought about, and I knew it was the best for me, and it had been on my mind for a long time. After a broken heart and trying to get over him, I kind of stayed to myself and kept my head in the books. I told myself I would never let another guy in my life, and I am going to shut them down if they try to talk to me.

I became bitter, hard, and numb. It's not my personality, carrying myself that way, but I felt safe with walls up and keeping others out. When your heart is broken, it will show in your attitude and how you carry yourself. So I was in school. I always sat in the back. I had been in school maybe about six months to a year. Really, I didn't care how I dressed for school. I dressed how I felt. I stayed to myself. At lunch time, I would eat in my car. As the months passed, I was trying to get over my pain. There was this young man who introduced himself to me. Really, I wasn't interested in him.

But, you know, he seemed to be a gentleman. Well, we started dating. We would study and hang out together. He seemed to be a nice guy, but I began to think I wanted someone who loved me for me. I decided that I needed to be loved. I don't have to change or measure up to be loved.

Yes! Single women will say they are looking for someone who is thoughtful, loyal, honest, and attractive. But you know deep down what most women want from that person, first and foremost, is to be accepted, appreciated, and admired. Maybe you can relate to what I am saying. I noticed he was trying to change me, but I was not going to have it. Not only was he in school, he also worked after school. He would ask me questions, like, "Can you cook?"

I would answer, "Yes!"

When I do not have a class, or I am not on campus. I did not live too far from the campus. I did invite him over a couple of times. My mother liked him, so that kind of made me like him too. Yes! Mom liked him, but I still had some trust issues. I made up my mind that I was going to look out for three of the powerful words.

1. Criticism. Most of us are sensitive to harsh and condemning words. Criticism always sends out a message that sends out a red flag.

2. Controlling behavior. It seems like in every woman relationship, especially a long-term relationship, you get remarkably close to someone. Most of the time, it is because of their own insecurity or insensitivity. You kind of know where this is going. But we seem to stay in the relationship. I guess we are searching.

3. Comparisons. Why? We have women who measure themselves in comparison with others. But you know we all have our own weaknesses and our own strengths. We need to stay in the liabilities where God has made us free.

John 8:36 (NIV) states, "So if the Son sets you free, you will be free indeed." We all need to know that it is only Jesus Christ who can make the difference.

After one of my study times with my boyfriend, it was getting late in the evening, and we were getting hungry. Later that day, I went to my boyfriend's house with some food. I just wanted to surprise him. So after getting off work, I went to my house and cooked for us. The food was good, and we watched TV. I realized, in his arms, I felt safe. I fell asleep. I was awakened out of my sleep with my boyfriend attacking me, trying to take my clothes off. There was no one around that could help me. He said, "DON'T *fight* IT!" *He kept trying to pull my pants off.*

I thought to myself, *Don't give up. You can do this. Keep fighting.* But he was much stronger than me. I began to say to myself, "*God, help!*" All of a sudden, I gained strength! I got away and ran to my car. I cranked up my car and drove away. With tears falling down my face, it came to me that he was going to rape me. You know, I am still having problems sleeping and have trust issues. I feel like demons are chasing me in my sleep. Fear tries to take control every now and then. I do thank God for a praying family and the support of my mother and father who loves me dearly. The most importing thing that I learned and am still learning is that I can inform other young women about date *rape*! To overcome any obstacle, I found out I must not let what happened in my past dictate my future.

By Lovelier Freedom

Falling Asleep

Wow! I was so excited when 2016 came. I just retired from the government, went full time in the women prison facility. Sometimes, excitement can get into the way of knowing what is your assignment that God is calling you to.

I loved going there every morning, three days out of the week. I decided to bring someone in one summer day as a visitor. I had been going there for maybe nine months.

I was teaching the women what it is to know what righteous living is. The visitor began to say unrighteous things to confuse the ladies. God kept me in control of the class without making a scene. I was so embarrassed, but I kept my cool.

I cannot really go into detail, but the outcome caused me to quit. I know what you are saying. How can you let one day out of the nine months make you quit?

It is like stacking up dominoes that took you nine months to set up, and they all came crashing down.

I prayed and moved on, waiting on what God wanted me to do in the kingdom. A young lady I knew decided to go on a mission. I did pray about it, and I was still waiting for the move of God to give me a go-ahead on this assignment. The assignment God called her to do was awesome! I was very happy to join her.

I would get up exceedingly early every morning to get ready. This was quite different from anything I had ever done. I believed that this was what made it exciting because it was different. In the year of 2017, things were going smoothly. Anything you are doing for God, you have to stay very watchful. In every believer's life, there will be some challenges. In those challenges, the Word of God should always be foremost on your mind to overcome anything. Now if you are not all the way devoted to Jesus Christ, you will fall for anything; you will be very much attracted to what you like. We are in the season where we must be incredibly careful in what society will expose us to, especially our children and grandchildren. We must keep our trust in God.

In the Midst of Your Season, Change Is Going to Come

And they overcame him by the blood of the
Lamb, and by the word of their testimony; and
they loved not their lives unto death.

—Revelation 12:11

There will always come a time in our life when it seems as if we are stuck and not moving in the direction where we know God is taking us. But as we continue to stay steadfast in God's Word, a change will come. Now I do not know when your change will come. It is all up to you.

There had been many times in my life I felt stuck and unworthy, even though I was a Christian. I felt drained and empty and sad. But the odd thing about it was God still uses me, and the ones that I minister to seemed to be going through the same thing that I was going through in my life.

Let the church say amen! When you realize it is not just you in the storms, you are enduring hardship as a good soldier for someone else.

Second Timothy 2:3–5 (NIV) says:

Join with me in suffering, like a
good soldier of Christ Jesus. No one serv-

ing as a soldier gets entangled in civilian affairs, but rather tries to please his commanding office. Similarly, anyone who competes as an athlete does not receive the victor's crown except by competing according to the rules.

So each of us has said, "Why does it seem like I am not getting ahead?"

God is omnipotent, has unlimited power. He is able to do everything as long as we suffer for Christ and not something we do because of unrighteousness. To keep walking in the Spirit of God, He will always be pleased with our life. It is such a blessing to help others than to think about us all the time. Let us keep changing every day that others shall see Christ in our walk. Galatians 5:16 states, "This I say then, walk in the Spirit, and ye shall not fulfill the lust of the flesh" (KJV).

Psalm 1:3 says, "And he shall be like a tree planted by the rivers of water, that bringeth forth his fruit in his season; his leaf also shall not wither and whatsoever he doeth shall PROSPER."

Prosper means to "flourish, thrive, growing strong."

In Jeremiah 17:8, at the end of the verse, it says, "Neither shall cease from yielding fruit."

Yielding means "giving way under pressure."

Pears takes three years to grow on a tree. Apples take two to four years and three to six years for maturity. Lemons consistently produce lemons every year. Some trees are slow growers (twenty to thirty years) to reach full size, and some grow fast, ten to fifteen years. Red maple (Acer rubrum) is a moderately fast grower; given good growing conditions, it should put on one to two feet of growth per year, once established.

How do trees grow leaves back?

Jeremiah identifies us as trees because we can identify with all four seasons. If a tree bud is green on the inside, they are alive and well, just waiting for their time to sprout. If you do not spot buds or the buds are shriveled up, that could indicate it is a problem.

Shriveled means "wrinkled and contracted, especially due to loss of moisture."

Ecclesiastes 3:1–8 (paraphrased) says, "To everything there is a Season and a time to every purpose under the heaven."

Genesis 8:22 states, "While the earth remained, Seedtime and harvest, and Cold and Heat, Summer and Winter, and day and night Shall not Cease."

Cease means "something coming to an end!" The hostilities had ceased, and normal life was resumed.

In the Midst of Your Season, Change Is Going to Come

There was a widow in 2 Kings 4:1–7 that Elisha helped, a poor widow. Second Kings 4:1–7 says:

> One day the widow of one of Elisha's fellow prophets came to Elisha and cried out to him, "My husband who served you is dead, and you know how he feared the Lord. But now a creditor has come, threatening to take my two sons as slaves."
>
> "What can I do to help you? Tell me, what do you have in the house?"
>
> "Nothing at all, except a flask (clay pot) of olive oil," she replied.
>
> And Elisha said, "Borrow as many empty jars as you can from your friends and neighbors. Then go into your house with your sons and shut the door behind you. Pour olive oil from your flask into the jars, setting the jars aside as they are filled."
>
> So she did as she was told, her sons brought many jars to her, and she filled

them one after another. Soon every container was full to the brim! "Bring me another jar," she said to one of her sons.

"There aren't any more!" he told her. And then the oil stopped flowing.

When she told the man of God what had happened, he said to her, "Now sell the olive oil and pay your debts, and there will be enough money left over to support you and your sons."

Hallelujah! Everything she needed was in the house. It takes one thing that will move the heart of God. Anytime God is in your house, you have more than enough. But first your faith must go along with what God is telling you to do. Go borrow some pots from your neighbors. By obeying the man of God, you are obeying God. Not only did she alone pay off her debt, but she also had more! Also, enough to substance her and your sons. God can bring you out of a poor situation.

So you may be the pear tree or apple tree. It does not matter how long you may go through the test. It's what you get out of the test. Maturity comes out when you want to learn.

When you think to yourself, *Why me?* the pain is real. I tell you one thing: it may hurt or you may think God does not hear you. There is a praise that pushes out of your Spirit that makes you bruise out with thanksgiving. Sometimes you will think you are all alone. Sometimes God will send someone by or you may be in church if the man or woman of God has a Word for you. It's still God, so just obey the Word that was spoken to you. First John 5:14–15 (KJV) says:

And this is the confidence that we have in him, that, if we ask anything

according to his will, he heareth you.
And if we know that he hears us, whatsoever we ask, we know that we have the
petitions that we desired for him.

How to Be an Overcomer and Soar Like an Eagle Women Conference 2019

But those that wait upon the Lord shall renew
their strength; they shall mount up with wings
as eagles; they shall run, and not be weary;
and they shall walk, and not faint.

—Isaiah 40:31

In our waiting there can be fullness of joy.

—Psalm 16:11

We sometimes do not feel strong. It most always takes hearing God's voice knowing that He loves us. And meditating on the goodness of God's promises, to reflect on where God has brought us out of. Amen.

Through the rough times, good times, quiet times, and alone times. *God is still good!* Amen.

Sometimes you may feel that you are hanging off a ledge without a bottom to catch you. But remember the Word of the Lord. He says that He will never leave you nor forsake you.

"Be strong and courageous. Do not be afraid or terrified because of them, for the LORD your God goes with you; he will never leave or forsake you" (Deuteronomy 31:6 NIV).

So while you are flying, your flying may be disappointment or sickness, maybe a runaway child. Keep flying! Keep moving in the things of God, even while you are flying. Hallelujah!

There have been times in my life I just could not get out of bed, feeling hurt with tears running down my face. My head would feel like it was going to burst.

Praying while I am crying, I am telling you there is something so powerful in praying to the Holy Spirit. He will not fail you. The floodgates just open wide with the word of knowledge, with understanding, and a release of burdens.

First Peter 5:7 (KJV) states, "Casting all your care upon him; for he cares for you." Knowing that God cares for you gives you so much confidence to trust Him while you wait. While waiting, we can walk it out, knowing that God has everything in control. *Don't stop praying!*

An eagle is a large bird with power and strength for its size with large wings, power in flight, and vision. As we are reminded of an eagle's strength, we can encourage ourselves to realize that we are far greater than any eagle, even though we can learn from its nature.

Has the Word of God stated to mount up with wings as an eagle? Let us continue in moving forward in our calling to where the Lord is taking us in our own seasons, and do not faint (getting tired) where we are heading in the kingdom of God. "Thy kingdom come thy will be done" (Luke 11:2 KJV).

So living here on earth, the kingdom of God will be done in us. Glory!

Staying strong in God and in His power outweighs all our problems. Second Corinthians 10:3–4 (RSV) says, "For though we live in the world we are not carrying on a worldly war, for the weapons of our warfare are not worldly but have divine power to destroy strongholds."

We sometimes struggle with strongholds in our life. It can be lying, not being a good steward of our finances, smoking, sex addiction, stealing, masking at church, fornication, masturbation, and infidelity. There is so much that believers are going through without telling someone about their strongholds (struggles). In time, we will learn through God that we can be an overcomer.

I thank God for the Word that is our road map to satisfaction as we take one day at a time.

Here are a few testimonies from some of the women:

The most enjoyable part of the women conference is how it seemed as if the women who were speaking were speaking into "my life, in my season." They spoke about how much power we had in our voice/presence, regardless of our gender. Just because we are women, wives, it does not limit us or hinder us to be able to carry our authority to be women of God!

—Ashley

As the first women conference, I loved the presence of God that filled the room. I feel like I grew so much as a woman of God, and I came out of my shell. As I was called to pray in the front, toward the end, I did not realize the impact it would have on me. This conference made me realize the power and gifts God gave me.

—Angie

Thank you, TSOTJM. Tonight, I confirmed God's power, strength, and love in my life. And it confirmed that God wants me to forgive my husband for forsaking me. God wants me to see him as a child of God. What a blessing. What a blessing! May your ministry be blessed.

—Susan

This was an amazing Holy Spirit service! These sisters have gifts in being sensitive to following the prompts of the Holy Spirit. Wow! This was an awesome, beautiful time in the Lord.

Lifting all these women of God in prayer. Mighty gifts in Him to share. Tonight, mighty speakers, mighty warriors, and ambassadors of Christ! Mighty lemon trees here!

I wish I could come back tomorrow. But I'll be with my babies and husband at our home church in Fredericksburg. Thank you for this truly awesome service.

—Name unknown

The conference was a real blessing! When I witnessed God working on hearts and minds and souls of His people, I was truly blessed. The gifts and blessings that God restored upon me and the anointing that He gave me was used to show my love to Him. Thank you, Pastor P. Russell, for the teaching that God allowed you to bring honor and glory to Himself.

—Name unknown

A Father Lacking in the Home

I was born in 1993 in Alexandria, Virginia, into a single-parent household with three siblings with me being the third. Growing up, I always knew that my father wasn't in the picture, but I did not know specifically where he was.

It was not until I remembered different seasons where my father would pop in and out of my life. My mother would take us to my grandmother's house to meet with him. We would meet and spend time with him, but I always remember feeling uneasy and uncomfortable around him.

After we would spend time with him, I noticed the visits would stop, and then a couple of years later, we would see him again. It was a continuous cycle. It was not until I got older that I realized my father was in and out of prison my entire life.

I did not like going to see my father, calling him Dad, or showing him love because I did not know him or love him. It was hard for me to connect with him as a father when I barely knew him.

It was hard for me to love someone I did not know. My mother raised me to be extraordinarily strong and independent, but I can see how the lack of a father figure affected and influenced me.

From dealing with rejection, lack of self-worth and identity, these are the types of issues that came into my life from my father not being in the house or having an active role in raising me.

It was not until I accepted Jesus Christ and entered a relationship with Him that my life was transformed, and I was able to be healed and restored from my past.

As of now, I have a bachelor's degree and my master's degree, and I have forgiven my father for not being in my life and helping my mom raise me.

Through my relationship with Jesus, I've been healed and restored, and God has used my past and will continue to use my past to influence and help others. Glory to God.

Name unknown

Looking Back

Since 1973, God has brought so many women in my life that were hurting in their walk of life. Some were believers, some were not. My soul rejoices knowing that the women that God had placed in my life had changed because of Jesus Christ.

Now I am preaching the Gospel of Jesus Christ, still teaching to broken women, when I once was a broken woman myself, having women conferences and round table talks, teaching them about intercessory prayer, teaching how to counsel other women, and mentoring.

The year 2020 was great! Pandemic to our country was hit with a disease called Coronavirus Many people have died, over five hundred thousand or maybe more. But in the pandemic, the revelation of God was shown to His people. God opened doors for His people to move into homes, open their own businesses, others gave their life to Jesus Christ, and healing was taking place. Even though everyone was wearing masks for protection, the Holy Spirit was moving among the land.

God's people were moving by God's Spirit, although we were obeying the law of the land by wearing our masks. God was still opening doors. There was a relationship being born, marriages taking place, and praise and worship, singing unto the Lord, new ministries taking place.

Now that we are in 2021, we are launching out, moving forward, excited in our new, where we are going in God's will.

In this pandemic, there were prophetic dreams that were spoken to me.

Birthing Taking Place in My Life

Another wow! There is always a test that comes to God's people to see if you will obey Him or someone else will.

A warning again from God! Be careful who lays hands on you! It can be a familiar face. God will always give you a way to escape a discernment (warning).

In the meantime, God had blessed me with a man of God that had added to my life. God will give him dreams about me.

This is what the *Lord* said to myself. In this dream, myself and my daughter were in a hospital room.

Dream one

This is what was spoken to me:
I had a dream in 2018. We were at the hotel doing ministry at the time.

In this dream, you and another young lady and I were in a hospital room. You were behind the curtain, but I still could see you as if my vision was looking through the curtain.

You were sitting in a chair next to the end of the bed, like someone who would help someone who was about to give birth.

In the dream, I felt like there were five children. I knew that meant that you would be a midwife in the ministry.

Dream two

Transitioning, rowing over. Hi, Mom! I had a dream about you. You said to me I am accepting hospital beds in my home, then I woke up.

I believe the dream is saying there is a shift in your ministry. Meaning, you are going to operate in the gift of healing, being obedient to the Lord, when called upon and directed by the Holy Spirit.

But now you are shifting into the ministry of healing.

Dream three

I had a dream that you and a friend of yours were around a large crowd of women. They were young adults and two older women. One table you were sitting at, the other table the other young lady was sitting at. You both were together. You were all under a white tent, like the one used for a revival service. Then I walked away and saw Dad with his dad and my siblings and their kids.

Dad was distributing food. I saw pancakes, then I went to grab a plate near me. Dad spoke to me and said that it was for Papa (granddad). Then I was told that I would have my own. I could see we were still under the tent.

Dad gave it to all his family's children and grandchildren. Then I woke up!

Dream four

I went walking on a long driveway. At the entry to my right were garbage bags of fresh vegetables. One vegetable I could see clearly were potatoes. I could tell one was mine at that time. I did not know the dream was about you.

I could tell the owner of the house was giving these out like one would to the needy. But I knew at that moment, there was a promise, like a promised blessing. I did not get what everyone else was getting but what has been stored up for me too. As I walked up the driveway and on the grass, to the side of the house, I saw an African tepee.

Now was the time that I could receive what rightfully belonged to me.

I saw Cicely Tyson walking from the tepee. She had this mantle over her head, and it fell off. She had long beautiful gray hair as she passed by me. I then said to myself, "This dream is about my mother." Then I heard the singer Mary sing, "You will see the goodness of the Lord and see them for the rest of your days, for your days will be long." Then I woke up.

Dream five

Shalom, women of God. The Lord said there is a revival anointing that you are about to step into. It has been on you since RW Schambach Ministry is about to come to its fulfillment.

You have given half territory, and the next generation carries the other half. This other half walks with them. It will be like Deborah. You will go with them. Young women and older women, you will rise up as a generation of revivalists. I hear the Lord also say, "You will see the glory of the ladder house." Amen!

Dream six

I had a dream that I was in most likely a building that was possibly a school and a dorm room. I don't know what a boarding school is, but I can assume it to be that.

I walked up to this window that had a desk in front of it and a desktop computer. My mother got on it, and she was beginning her Zoom session. It seems like she arrived in Jerusalem while being in the US.

I would say Jerusalem because I could sense that the program she was on was like TBN and ACIJ approved things, but it was live, like someone being on Facebook.

I could see the numbers of individuals watching. There were 945 and going up.

I was like, "Mom, this is great! You need to get started and ready because they are waiting for you."

I also felt like on that channel, it was something to do with having the heart cry of aborted children and a calling of repentance. It seemed like everyone was judged for how many children that didn't have a chance of life. *Lord, I receive* (Joel 2:28)!

Get Up and Move!

You know there was a time when I felt stuck. What I mean about that was it seemed like some tests came to shake my faith. If you don't know what I am talking about, then something is wrong. Check your walk in Christ.

I like basketball, especially doing a slam dunk. How about you? If you don't stay focused, the enemy will block your dunk. He (devil) doesn't want you to stay focused on what your assignment is in the season God has designed for you to carry out.

Matthew 18:6 (KJV) says, "But whoso shall offend one of these little ones which believe in me, it was better for him that a millstone was hung about his neck, and that he was drowned in the depth of the sea."

Jesus cares how you treat others, restaurant waitresses, and others that are low-income servers, leaders.

Romans 12:16 states, "Be of the same mind one toward another. Mind not high things but condescend to men of low estate. Be not wise in your own conceits."

I don't have time for that! I have to do what God calls me to do, to encourage others, to lay hands on the sick, raise the dead. We think raising the dead is just the human body. No! It is also the person who is spiritually dead. Raise them up and set them free. Glory to God!

It was good that I was afflicted. It made me strong. I'm back! Some thought I wasn't going to make it. They thought because I was abominable, she's weak, she cannot think clearly, she's crying, she's all alone. Not so! I have landed back on my feet. Elevation, worshiping, strategy, interceding, and a watchful eye.

Matthew 26:41 (KJV) says, "Watch and pray, that ye enter not into temptation: the Spirit indeed is willing, but the flesh is weak."

God wants our heart to flow. Don't let forgiveness stop the flow of God in your life.

Isaiah 59:19 (KJV) states, "So shall they fear the name of the Lord from the west, and his glory from the rising of the sun. When the enemy shall come in like a flood, the Spirit of the Lord shall lift a standard against him."

God is always on my side, protecting me.

Second Timothy 4:18 (KJV) says, "And the Lord shall deliver me from every evil work and will preserve me unto his heavenly kingdom; to whom be glory for ever and ever. Amen."

So if I let something get in my heart, it will stomp my growth because it will slow me down, and that's not how God made me. I cannot let anything shut down my vision, always keeping my heart open. I will not let know one stop what God is doing, and I will let God fight my battles. I cannot let anything slow me down. I will not look at the person's actions because the enemy wants me to interpret what I see.

God, I will trust you! God, I trust you! This will work out for my good.

So loose the lies, loose the curse, loose your freedom, loose the disappointments. Let God be your voice! In the name of Jesus.

Where We Belong

We belong in the kingdom. Jesus said in John 14:2 (KJV), "In my Father's house there are many mansions; if it was not so, I would have told you I would go to prepare a place for you."

We don't belong here on this earth. Yes, we have been living here all our life. When we gave our lives to Jesus Christ, He made us a promise to prepare a place for us. How would you feel if you had been living for God, doing His will, and you would never see the God who started all of this from the beginning? Let us all make it to heaven.

He's a Father who takes care of His child. Just think while we're on earth, He's building us a home to live.

God is a promise keeper; He also says in His Word, Numbers 23:19 (KJV), "God is not a man, that He should lie; neither the Son of man, that he should repent: hath he said, and shall he not do it? or hath he spoken, and shall he not make it good?"

So while we are waiting here on earth, we are not of this world.

John 15:19 (KJV) says, "If ye were of the world, the world would love his own: but because ye are not of the world, but I have chosen you out of the world therefore the world hateth you."

Some may think it is hard to live in this world that God has created for us. We didn't know who our Creator was (God). It was easy to live in this world. Why? Because we were born here, John 15:19 (KJV) says, "If ye were of the world, the world would love his own: but because ye are not of the world, therefore the world hateth you." Living here, we have so much in common—sin! That's why the Word of God tells us after we have given our life to God, becoming a Christian, we are no longer attached to the activities that take place in an ungodly manner (world).

Romans 6:1–2 (KJV) states, "What shall we say then? Shall we continue in sin, that grace may abound? God forbid. How shall we, that are dead to sin, live any longer therein?"

The Glory of God Came into the Room

What a mighty God we serve! I don't know why we as believers can see with our natural eyes when a person is not feeling well (sick) but cannot discern in the Holy Spirit when a person has been restrained by the enemy. We must do better by being sensitive in the Holy Spirit. We should walk by faith every day.

Second Corinthians 5:7 (KJV) says, "For we walk by faith, not by sight." Then we can see with our spiritual eyes, doing the will of the Father.

John 8:36 (KJV) states, "If the Son therefore shall make you free, ye shall be free indeed."

We must get back doing our Father's business, being a disciple and making disciples.

Disciple: a follower or student of a teacher, a personal follower of Jesus during his life.

We should always be ready, more than going to work, laying our clothes out at night, impressing our boss. Always be ready to spread the good news.

Matthew 6:33 (KJV) says, "But seek ye first the kingdom of God, and his righteousness; and all these things shall be added unto you." Seeking God first makes our morning run so smooth, preparing ourselves for the day. When we live in the realm of God, we will find ourselves seeking to do

71

God's will while starting our day also. How do you start your day? Do you start by looking at your cell phone? Or dropping to your knees with thanksgiving?

What a wonderful way to start your morning, seeking the Lord, feeling His presence, and the anointing moving in your room.

You may be saying, "That never happens to me." Just keep seeking the face of God. Your relationship will begin to change while you keep walking with Him.

John 15:27 (KJV) states, "And ye also shall bear witness, because ye have been with me from the beginning."

I don't know the day or year you have given your life to Jesus Christ, the Son of God. Make your first steps toward joyfulness, full of smiles, fulfillment, and excitement! Or maybe like me, God healed me the same time I accepted Jesus Christ as my Lord and Savior. Stay on this journey, this path called for freedom.

Can we take some time out now and give God some praise? Hallelujah!

You cannot talk about the Lord without getting excited with joy, feeling His love, knowing the faith of God, God's faithfulness, God's love, God's plan, God's protection.

How to Know Your Enemy

The Bible says in John 10:10 (KJV), "The thief cometh not, but for to steal, and to kill, and destroy I am (Jesus) come that they might have life, and that they might have it more abundantly."

Let's break down *might*. What's the word telling us?

1. Strength
2. Force
3. Power

Primarily supernatural power, strength, or as to work or strive with all of one's might. Reading the Word of God, in this verse, lets us know not to be fools of the devil.

Second Corinthians 2:11 (KJV) says, "Lest Satan should get advantage of us: for we are not ignorant of his devices."

Second Corinthians 2:11 (NIV) states, "In order that Satan might not outwit us. For we are not unaware of his schemes."

Do you know that Satan's devices can be a disobedient child? Or bring disagreement in a marriage? Or bring discord on your job, infidelity in a marriage, and many other things he attacks us with?

We must always watch and pray, whether we are at church, out fellowshipping with saints, or the corporate world.

Everyone that goes to church doesn't mean they have given their life to Christ. According to 1 John 1:9 (KJV), it states, "If we confess our sins, he (Jesus) is faithful and just to forgive us our sins and to cleanse us from all unrighteousness."

Do you not know people love going to church? They like the music, how it makes them feel, and the preaching. They call it catching the Holy Ghost because of the feeling he or she feels. When church is over, they still live the same way that they came to church. It's called religious!

You must have discernment. Discernment means Christianity. The word may have several meanings.

Discernment can *describe the process of determining God's desire in a situation or for one's life or identifying the true nature of a thing*, such as discerning whether a thing is good, evil, or may even transcend the limiting notion of duality.

Many of us have testimonies of when we were young in the Lord, so happy to be saved, loving God, and trusting everyone, not knowing that you can run into so many problems of others that are not Christlike, not living God's lifestyle.

Romans 8:3–5 (KJV) says:

> For what the law could not do, in that it was weak through, the flesh, God sending his Son in the likeness of sinful flesh, and for sin, condemned sin in the flesh: That the righteousness of the law might be fulfilled in us, who walk not after the flesh but after the Spirit.
>
> For they that are after the flesh do mind the things of the flesh; but they that are after the Spirit the things of the Spirit.

So let us be aware of Satan's devices, and if you should walk into a trap, pass the test so you never would have to take the test again.

Let's pray. Heavenly Father, when trouble comes to us, let us be reminded of what your Word says in 1 John 1:9. In Jesus's name. Amen.

A Call to Return to God

Romans 7:18–25 (KJV) states:

> For I know that in me (that is, in my flesh,) dwelleth no good thing: for to will is present with me; but how to perform that which is good I find not.

> For the good that I would I do not: but the evil which I would not, that I do.

> Now if I do that I would not, it is no more I that do it, but sin that dwelleth in me.

> I find then a law, that, when I would do good, evil is present with me.

> For I delight in the law of God after the inward man:

> But I see another law in my members, warring against the law of my mind, and bringing me into captivity to the sin which is in my members.

> O wretched man that I am! Who shall deliver me from the body of this death?

> I thank God through Jesus Christ our Lord. So then with the mind I serve the law of God, but with the flesh the law of sin.

We must keep our mind clean daily and have a prayer life and, for most, reading and studying in the Word of God. Also, we must know that the old man, which is the flesh of man, will always try to rise. That's why it's very important who we fellowship with. How many times have we fallen into a trap of the enemy because we thought that he or she was a Christian? And we didn't see any fruit.

Galatians 5:22–23 (KJV) states: "But the fruit of the Spirit is love, joy peace, longsuffering, gentleness, goodness, faith, Meekness, temperance, against such there is no law."

Why? Do you think a Man or Woman of God says to watch a person (Fruit). Because of this, let us know the character of a person walking in Christ Jesus to discern the Spirit of God character.

When I Was a Child

From the time we were little girls playing with our dolls, we wanted to be wives and a mother. We would play house with our bobbie dolls, tea sets, and our play food.

If you are coming from a home with both parents, your parents were your role models, gleaming what marriage looks like with a man and woman.

Now that you become a woman, you don't think about that so much, but the dream is still real.

It was a day I was traveling, the weekend of Mother's Day. The sun was shining, a little chill in the air. My mind was so much focused on my life, in what I have done that God wasn't pleased with.

There was a heavy presence that came upon me that I have felt many times before, a good peaceful calm present. I knew that God heard me while in my quiet times of confessions. I repented to Him with a sorrowful heart, and I am so much more joyful than I have ever been.

Name unknown

It's the Most Wonderful World!

In February 2022, I traveled to South Korea. My experience in South Korea started with feeling homesick. I decided to travel in the month of February of 2022 to go visit or spend some time with my husband who worked as a security contractor in South Korea.

In South Korea, winter has thin air, and it is very cold. I did love the winter, but I was really looking forward to spring.

Getting out of the apartment, I found out that South Koreans were very friendly, and they worked very hard, especially the elders.

My husband, being a military retiree, we lived on the economy but had all rights on the military base facility. I felt right at home when I was on base, with the men and women in their uniforms.

I will never forget my experience as a military wife., and raising our children of seven and meeting new friends and traveling. I loved it!

I was in South Korea for nine months and back at home now in the US. There's no place like home.

A Father's Love

April 18, 1922–January 25, 2010

Wow! Where should I start? I guess from the beginning. My father was born on April 18, 1922, in Nashville County, North Carolina, raised by both of his parents, Walter Gray Collins and Leah Pearson Collins. Daddy had five brothers and four sisters. There were ten of them.

My dad lived a hard life, but there was one thing he taught me: love and what love looks like.

He taught me to show love in action, not just saying I love you but also demonstrating love. My mommy and daddy were givers. That's how I learned to have the gift of giving.

Daddy's personality was a quiet man, very observant, and learning from other people, and he could laugh so loud.

Oh, how I miss his laughter! We would laugh just because he was laughing.

We sat up many days and nights talking about the past, present, and future. He taught me what it was to be a little girl, a teenager, and a woman. Oh, how I miss my daddy. Don't get it twisted. I miss my mommy too. I think about her a lot also. I love you, Mommy.

I could see my daddy coming down the block by looking out the window. We lived on the fifth floor in a brownstone building in New York City (in Harlem, Manhattan).

I could still hear his keys jingling as he was coming up the stairs. I would wait for him every night. "What did you do today, Daddy? Daddy, how was your day today?" I was about ten years old at that time.

Dad was a strong Black man working three jobs, but you know, the funniest thing was he never said, "I'm tired."

Daddy never complained at any time. Remember, I was ten; I guess he had a pillow talk with Mommy.

He was always ready to hear about my day, and how I listened to my mother doing my day.

At that time, I had two brothers, Alvin Collins, and my youngest brother, Terry Collins. Terry transferred on November 9, 2018. I miss you, Terry.

Daddy loved people. I guess I can say I got that from him and Mommy. And could he eat! He was a little man! But, boy, could he eat! Out of all the meats, beef, turkey, pork, Daddy loved his chicken!

When it was time to eat, we could hear my daddy humming. He knew what time it was.

It didn't take much to please him. He was always thinking about what he could do for others. My dad was a Southern man and always started out his words first. "Tricia, you know what happened?" He would make me laugh because he was going to say, "I'm not lying!"

My dad was a Christian man. He didn't like to be around liars, but he would give anybody the benefit of the doubt. Daddy gave his life to Jesus Christ at the age of seventy-two.

It was a refreshing time for Dad. I told him that Jesus loved him, and "you cannot get into the kingdom of heaven without asking Jesus Christ into your heart" (1 John 1:9, paraphrased).

So Dad and I walked the Christian journey together. He became a deacon in his church, working in the church without knowing Jesus Christ as his personal Savior.

The good news was Dad really knew the meaning of servitude, being a servant in the kingdom.

Titus 3:5–7 states:

> Not by works of righteousness which we have done, but according to his mercy he saved us, by the washing of regeneration, and renewing of the Holy Ghost.
>
> Which he shed on us abundantly through Jesus Christ our Savior.
>
> That being justified by his grace, we should be made heirs according to the hope of eternal life.

I thank God that I had a close relationship with my dad. It reminds me of the spiritual relationship that I have with the heavenly Father, communicating with God all the time. *Only*!

One thing Dad could not do was to die for my sins. It took the blood of Jesus Christ dying on the cross for the remission of my sins (the cancellation of debt, charge, or penalty).

Hebrews 9:22 says, "And almost all things are by the law purged with blood; and without shedding of blood is no remission."

Hebrews 9:28 states, "So Christ was once offered to bear the sins of many; and unto them that look for him shall he appear the second time without sin unto salvation."

My tribute to my daddy, Walter Leo Collins.

My Beloved Brother

October 12, 1957–November 9, 2018

With tears in my eyes, I want to acknowledge my youngest brother, Terry Leo Collins. Only someone like me knows what it feels like to lose a sibling or mother and father, and I have lost all three.

I miss our long talks and outings, just going shopping or going out for breakfast or lunch, just staying in; I would cook breakfast or dinner. I would ask Terry if the meals tasted good. He would say, "Why would you ask me that, Pat? You know it tastes good!"

Terry Leo Collins was known as brother, son, husband, Dad, Daddy, Unc, Uncle T, and Uncle Terry. My brother took his titles very seriously.

He was very special to us and everyone he met.

My brother went into the military on November 24, 1975. Terry was stationed at Fort Bragg, North Carolina. I want to take time out now to salute him by thanking my brother for his service.

Terry was always helpful in giving when it was needed. I guess you can say that's a legacy that our parents left us and hard work ethics. My brother would go to the food banks and take food to the residents that lived in his apartment building. My brother had his struggles in many areas of his life but still had a kind heart. I was always talking to him about Jesus Christ, how life was great in Christ Jesus.

He would go to church with me, and I would watch him across the room while he was listening to the preacher. I was praying to my heavenly Father that salvation would come to him on that day. Well, it didn't happen that Sunday, but I kept my trust in God.

Romans 13:11–13 says:

> And that, knowing the time, that now is high time to awake out of sleep: for now, is our salvation nearer than when we believed.
>
> The night is far spent, the day is at hand: let us therefore cast off the works of darkness and let us put on the armor of light.
>
> Let us walk honestly, as in the day, not in rioting and drunkenness, not in chambering and wantonness, not in strife and envying.

Before my brother closed his eyes, he gave his life to Jesus Christ. God also healed my brother of liver disease before he had even given his life to Christ. Hallelujah!

I always looked forward to our rides from Fredericksburg, Virginia, us going to church in Loudoun County, Virginia.

We sang, we prayed, we encouraged one another, and sometimes God's presence was so powerful! We worshipped! Read Philippians 4:4–9.

When we go through life's storms, we should ask God for guidance and ask Him not only to give us strength but also to seek deliverance. We must keep a positive attitude.

If negative thoughts start to bombard us with destructive thoughts, we have to shake them off immediately.

The Scriptures state to have pure, lovely, good, virtuous thoughts. This can be achieved by counting our blessings and keeping our mind stayed on Christ (Philippians 4:10–19, paraphrased).

During our lifetimes, we had plenty, and we have experienced lack.

Through both circumstances, the Lord has blessed us in many ways. Count your blessings, and I'm sure you will find hope and joy.

Written on Sunday, July 26, 2009, by my brother, Terry L Collins

Message from the Author

Greetings in the name of Jesus Christ. I pray that you would enjoy this book, that this book would give you insight on the ratio of teen pregnancy, or maybe you will find yourself in some of these short stories, feeling the presence of God in your room or workplace.

My mission for writing this book is to help all women around the globe to know their potential in having developed whatever they become in the future, freedom from sabotage, isolation, disappointments, rejection, abandonment, and a broken heart.

About the Author

Greetings in the name of our *Lord Jesus Christ*. My name is Patricia L. Collins Russell.

I was born in Goldsboro, North Carolina. At the age of six, my parents moved to New York City. That was where I was raised. I am the eighth child out of twelve children. I accepted Jesus Christ as my personal Savior at the age of eighteen in Brooklyn, New York, on October 1973. I am a mother of seven adult children and eighteen grandchildren. I have been married for forty-nine years, and this year, 2023, will be our fiftieth anniversary.

God began to use me in New York City. I began to hand out Christian tracts. My husband is a retired army. He served in Brooklyn, New York, at Fort Hamilton Army Base, and traveled to countries around the world.

I became an evangelist in 1984, then I was ordained as a minister in 2007 and a pastor in 2018.

I pray that you would enjoy this book, that this book would give you insight on the ratio of teen pregnancy, or maybe see yourself in some of these stories, feeling the presence of God in your room or workplace.

My mission for writing this book is to help all women around the globe to know their potential in having developed whatever they become in the future, freedom from sabotage, isolation, disappointments, rejection, abandonment, and a broken heart.